★ ★ ★ ★ ★ ★ **MILITARY FAMILIES** ★ ★ ★ ★ ★ ★

My Uncle Is in the
AIR FORCE

SAM CAULKINS

PowerKiDS
press

New York

Published in 2016 by The Rosen Publishing Group, Inc.
29 East 21st Street, New York, NY 10010

First Edition

Editor: Sarah Machajewski
Book Design: Katelyn Heinle/Tanya Dellaccio

Photo Credits: Cover, pp. 5 (airman), 22 © iStockphoto.com/tonylarson; cover backdrop, p. 1 David Smart/Shutterstock.com; pp. 3–4, 6, 8, 10, 12, 14, 16, 18, 20, 22, 24 (camouflage texture) Casper1774/Shutterstock.com; pp. 7 (both), 9 (top), 11, 13, 15 (both), 17, 21 courtesy of U.S. Air Force Flickr; p. 9 (bottom) Monkey Business Images/Shutterstock.com; p. 19 (top) Hank Shiffman/Shutterstock.com; p. 19 (bottom) Straight 8 Photography/Shutterstock.com.

Library of Congress Cataloging-in-Publication Data

Caulkins, Sam, author.
 My uncle is in the Air Force / Sam Caulkins.
     pages cm. — (Military families)
 Includes index.
 ISBN 978-1-5081-4455-7 (pbk.)
 ISBN 978-1-5081-4446-5 (6 pack)
 ISBN 978-1-5081-4456-4 (library binding)
 1. United States. Air Force—Juvenile literature. I. Title.
 UG633.C366 2015
 358.400973—dc23
                                    2015036309

Manufactured in the United States of America

CPSIA Compliance Information: Batch #BW16PK: For Further Information contact Rosen Publishing, New York, New York at 1-800-237-9932

CONTENTS

All About My Uncle

I have a really cool uncle. He's my dad's brother, and we do a lot of fun things together. He's not just my uncle—he's also an airman in the United States Air Force.

The U.S. Air Force is an important branch of our country's military. The men and women who serve in this branch do a lot to **protect** our country and its citizens. I remember when my uncle joined the air force because it wasn't that long ago. It can be hard to have a family member in the military, but it also makes me very proud.

★★★

Military Matters

Men and women who serve in the air force are called airmen.

JOINING THE MILITARY IS A BIG DECISION, OR CHOICE.
MY UNCLE IS VERY BRAVE FOR JOINING.

THE FIVE BRANCHES

The U.S. military is one of the biggest and most powerful militaries the world. It's made of five branches. The branches are the air force, army, coast guard, navy, and Marine **Corps**.

The air force is responsible for **missions** that take place in the air. Some people may think all airmen do is fly planes, but that isn't true. The air force carries out **aerial** attacks on enemies. It also **defends** the United States against aerial attacks from enemies. The air force helps with search-and-rescue missions, carries needed supplies to other countries, and carries out space research.

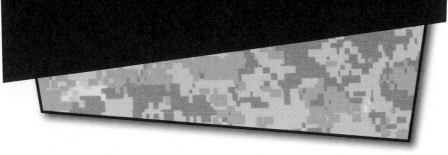

THE AIR FORCE WORKS WITH THE OTHER BRANCHES OF THE MILITARY TO KEEP THE UNITED STATES AND ITS PEOPLE SAFE.

The History of the Air Force

The U.S. military started using aircraft soon after airplanes were invented. The first group that was like the air force formed in 1907. It fought bravely during World War I. During World War II, what was then called the Army Air Forces operated as part of the U.S. Army. About 2.4 million airmen helped the United States win the war.

In 1947, the U.S. Air Force finally became an independent branch. As of 2014, there were around 330,000 active-duty airmen in the air force. "Active duty" means they work for the air force full time.

★★★
Military Matters
The air force has a special group called the Air Force Reserve. Reserve airmen are part-time airmen. They're ready to serve when they're needed.

ACTIVE-DUTY AIRMAN

RESERVE AIRMAN

MY UNCLE IS AN ACTIVE-DUTY AIRMAN. HIS FULL-TIME JOB IS WORKING FOR THE AIR FORCE. RESERVE AIRMEN SERVE IN THE AIR FORCE, BUT THEY OFTEN HAVE OTHER JOBS, TOO.

JOINING THE AIR FORCE

My uncle chose to join the air force after high school. First, he had to meet the requirements. To join the air force, a person has to be between 17 and 39 years old. They have to be a U.S. citizen or must have lawfully entered the country. They must have a high school **diploma**. The air force also takes people who have a GED, which is much like a high school diploma.

Then, my uncle had to pass a health exam and a test called the ASVAB. This test asks questions about math and reading. The ASVAB helps future airmen figure out what career they'll have in the air force.

MOST PEOPLE WORK WITH A RECRUITER BEFORE ENLISTING IN, OR JOINING, THE MILITARY. A RECRUITER HELPS PEOPLE DECIDE IF JOINING THE MILITARY IS RIGHT FOR THEM. MY UNCLE'S RECRUITER ANSWERED ALL THE QUESTIONS MY FAMILY HAD ABOUT SERVING IN THE AIR FORCE.

Becoming an Airman

After my uncle enlisted, he had to leave for Basic Military Training (BMT). It's held in San Antonio, Texas. Training lasts for around eight weeks, and it can be really hard. My uncle said he had to wake up at 5:00 a.m. to run!

During training, **recruits** do drills and learn the skills they need to serve in the air force. They learn how to be **disciplined** and how to work as part of a team. After eight weeks, my uncle graduated. He earned the Air Force Airman's Coin, which showed he was finally an airman.

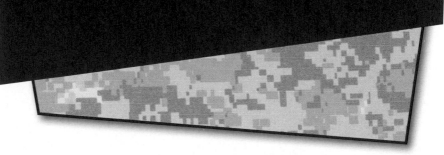

MY FAMILY MISSED MY UNCLE WHEN HE WAS AT TRAINING. HE KNEW THAT HE HAD OUR SUPPORT BACK HOME. WE WERE VERY PROUD OF HIM WHEN HE GRADUATED!

Heading to Technical School

My uncle went to **technical** training after basic training. Here, he learned how to do his job with the air force. Each career field has its own technical school. My uncle chose to be an air traffic controller, so he trained at a school in Mississippi.

My uncle said technical school was like regular school. He took classes and had to pass tests. However, it was different from regular school because he did a lot of hands-on training. For example, he learned how to operate the computers air traffic controllers use every day. His training lasted more than two months, but some technical training can last up to two years.

IT TAKES A LOT OF TRAINING TO BE IN THE AIR FORCE! AIRMEN TAKE CLASSES AND DO A LOT OF HANDS-ON WORK. ALL THE TRAINING MAKES THE U.S. AIR FORCE ONE OF THE STRONGEST AIR FORCES IN THE WORLD.

A Career with the Air Force

My uncle loves being an air traffic controller. He gets to direct the aircraft that come to and leave from an air force base, which you'll learn about later. He makes sure all the aircraft have enough time and room to take off and land safely. He talks to pilots and studies the weather. He also helps out in emergencies.

This isn't the only career the air force offers. The air force has pilots, airmen who serve in **combat**, nurses, **equipment** experts, security forces, and more. These careers teach skills that can be used after people leave the air force.

THIS AIRMAN PREPARES EQUIPMENT TO BE USED IN AN AIR FORCE MISSON. HE LEARNED HOW TO USE THIS EQUIPMENT DURING TRAINING.

My Uncle's Life

My uncle lives on an air force base. A base is where the air force keeps its equipment. Bases are much like regular neighborhoods, except everyone who lives there is in the air force or has a family member who is. Air force bases have homes, stores, libraries, schools, and parks. There's also an airport, of course!

The air force base is far from my family's home. I don't get to see my uncle every day, so I miss him a lot. However, we talk on the phone and over the computer. I can also go visit him whenever I want!

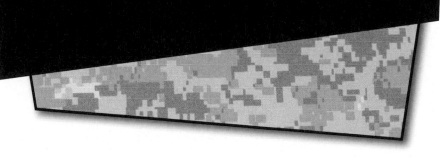

MY UNCLE'S LIFE IS JUST LIKE MY PARENTS'. HE WORKS DURING THE DAY. AFTER WORK, HE MAKES DINNER, SPENDS TIME WITH HIS FRIENDS, AND DOES EVERYDAY STUFF, SUCH AS WATCHING TV AND READING.

WHAT IS DEPLOYMENT?

I'm proud of my uncle for being in the military. His job isn't easy. One time, he had to leave home to serve overseas. This is called deployment. Many air force families think deployment is the hardest part of their family member's job.

When my uncle was deployed, he had to serve in another country for a few months. Some deployments last more than a year. During deployment, airmen may face dangerous, or unsafe, events. We worried about my uncle when he was deployed, and we missed him. I was happy when he came home safe.

MY UNCLE SAID THAT MY FAMILY'S SUPPORT WAS VERY IMPORTANT DURING HIS DEPLOYMENT. IT MADE HIM FEEL BETTER TO KNOW THERE WERE PEOPLE BACK HOME WHO LOVE AND SUPPORT HIM. WE WERE SO HAPPY WHEN HE CAME HOME!

MILITARY HEROES

I'm proud of my uncle because he chose to serve our country. Because of airmen, our country is a safer place to live. Not everyone can do my uncle's job. I think he's very brave.

If you have a family member in the air force, you may feel like your family is different from other families. However, it's really special to be part of a military family. Your family member isn't just part of your family. They're a hero, too. My uncle will always be my hero!

GLOSSARY

aerial: Having to do with being in the air.

combat: Fighting between armed forces.

corps: A group within a branch of a military organization that does a particular kind of work.

defend: To keep safe.

diploma: A piece of paper that shows somebody has finished a certain level of schooling.

disciplined: Having controlled behavior.

equipment: The objects needed for a certain purpose.

mission: An important job.

protect: To keep safe.

recruit: A person new to the armed forces who is not yet fully trained.

technical: Having to do with applied sciences.

Index

Websites

Due to the changing nature of Internet links, PowerKids Press has developed an online list of websites related to the subject of this book. This site is updated regularly. Please use this link to access the list: www.powerkidslinks.com/mili/airf